Thoughts of The Mind

A selection of poems for children

Jackie Fisher

Dedicated to my grandchildren Caleb and Ava. Always remember you can achieve the impossible.

Dear Reader

These poems have been created from suggested topics provided by children aged 6-11.

Each poem comes with a statement to encourage you to be the best you can be. There is also a page for you to express how you feel and maybe create a poem of your own. If you decide to create a masterpiece, I would love you to share it with me.

With your permission, I will display your creation on my website in the Children's Corner under Poem of The Month.

Your poem can be sent to: jaypoems2020@gmail.com

I hope you enjoy my book, and it inspires you to be creative.

Happy reading

Jackie Fisher

Selection of poems

I Wish 6

Imagine 9

The Adventure 12

The Open Book 15

Just Me..18

Launch Pad... 20

Friendships... 24

The Gamer.. 27

When I Grow Up.. 30

A Day Out... 33

I Wish

"Don't be afraid to wish BIG".

I Wish

Sometimes I wish I could eat all the ice cream in the world without getting a brain freeze.

Sometimes I wish I can go to school and be different without being teased.

Sometimes I wish I could be brave and tell my friends how good friendships should be.

Sometimes I wish my friends would just accept me for me.

Sometimes I wish someone would take a moment to ask why I am feeling so sad.

Sometimes I wish someone would encourage me to express myself, so I can share why I am feeling so mad.

Sometimes I wish.......

How are you feeling after reading I Wish?

Create your own poem.

Imagine

"When you imagine, you open up a world of possibilities".

Imagine

Can you imagine yourself as a dinosaur?

Which dinosaur would you choose to be?

Would you have a long tail and neck like a Diplodocus
so you could feast on a tree?

How about a Tyrannosaurus Rex?

You would be the most ferocious predator in your
neighbourhood as you parade along your street.

Showing off your huge jaws and sharp teeth to every
person you meet.

Or maybe a Pterosaurs so you can spread your wings
as you soar through the sky.

With the wind on your face and you thinking how
great it is to be able to fly.

You could consider being a Stegosaurus displaying
your

diamond-shaped bony plates on your back.

Swinging your spiked tail from side to side, leaving
everything behind you in a stack.

How are you feeling after reading Imagine?

Create your own poem.

The Adventure

"Make positive memories."

The Adventure

The swings are exciting as I get pushed to and fro. I hear an adult say to a child "Here we go!"

As I request for the swing to go higher and higher, my stomach fills with butterflies and strands of my hair stand to attention like wire.

As the swing takes its time to slow down for me to get out, I have already decided my next adventure to be the roundabout.

It comes to a standstill and now safe to get on. All my friends come and join me, Caleb, Ava, Alfie and John.

What fun we are having going around and around as the speed is getting faster. "Hold on tight, everyone! We definitely don't want a disaster!"

Next, we explore the climbing frame while we have a quick game of Tag. The winner claims their victory when they raise the flag.

Such a busy day filled with laughter and fun, it is time to go inside. "Hey! Caleb, Ava, Alfie and John, let's have one more go on the slide".

How are you feeling after reading The Adventure?

Create your own poem.

The Open Book

"You can never have too much knowledge."

The Open Book

As I turned the page, this mythical creature comes alive in front of my eyes. Mouth wide open, unable to blink, as I am stunned into a moment of surprise.

The horn swirls colours like a rainbow and the mane sparkles like glitter. Eyes so bright like a shining star with every blink creating its own glimmer.

My heart beats faster as the wings expand and casts an amazing shadow on the ground. Each flutter brings a gust of wind, keeping me firmly to the ground.

The clip-clopping sound of the hoofs is crystal clear as it prances around showcasing its colourful tail. With a hop and leap, it returns to the page giving me the perfect moment to inhale.

How are you feeling after reading The Open Book?

Create your own poem.

Just Me

"Loving yourself is just as important as liking your friends".

Just Me

When you look in the mirror, what do you see?

I see no one else but me!

I like the fact I can style my hair in so many unique ways.

My favourite style, if done well, can last for days and days.

My long eyelashes I like the best as they prevent the dust from getting into my big brown eyes.

What is most important to me is how I feel inside.

My lips are plump which I really like as they make my smile look awesome!

I appreciate the way I look because that is all that matters.

To be me is something exceptionally great and that is my number one factor.

When you look in the mirror, what do you see?

I see no one else but me!

How are you feeling after reading Just Me?

Create your own poem.

Launch Pad

"*Always aim high.*"

Launch Pad

5....4....3....2...1... Lift-off!

As we launch into the unknown, the feeling of dizziness takes over. A slight sensation of a stomach upset disappears as we embrace composure.

With us travelling more than 20 times the speed of sound, approximately 18,000 miles per hour. The anticipation becomes intense with our rocket consuming all the power.

The landing gear has been released with the spacecraft landing with a thrust and drag. We are incredibly happy to have arrived safely and even more excited about planting our flag.

We are surrounded by total silence, different-sized rocks and powder-like dust. As we slowly attempt to take our steps, it takes us time to adjust.

A float less bizarre feeling is present in every step we try to take.

That awesome feeling we get with every successful footprint we make.

How are you feeling after reading Launch Pad?

Create your own poem.

Friendships

"Friends should value you as you would value them."

Friendships

Friends are all different shades and sizes, with many full of funny jokes and surprises.

Friends support each other in every single way, helping one another day after day.

Friends will encourage, friends will rejoice, friends will defend you when you no longer can find your voice.

Friends can be thoughtful, caring and kind, listening to you while you share with them what is on your mind.

Friends may disagree, argue and cry about many different things, and never forget what joy true friendships bring.

How are you feeling after reading Frienships?

Create your own poem.

The Gamer

"Always try to have as much fun as you can."

The Gamer

I sit so comfortably in your hands and feel you
holding onto my unit quite tight. I hear your
triumphant cheer as you squeeze me with all your
might.

The last two laps have been really tough, but you've
managed to stay in first place. Not too fast around
the next bend, you do not want to lose this race.

Your mind tells you, "Press left, press left!" But
without thinking, you press right. Oh dear! Cars 10
and 7 are now completely out of sight.

You automatically correct the error to get yourself
back in the race. Your thumb connects with the
joystick and you quickly pick up the pace.

The big white flag in the distance indicates one more
lap to go. Unsure which move to make next, you
observe my acceleration button glow.

With one push of the button, you speed right past
players number 7 and 10. The victory is ours as we
receive a prize taking first place again.

How are you feeling after reading the Gamer?

Create your own poem.

When I Grow Up

"You can achieve the impossible."

When I grow up

When I grow up, what could I be?

I could be a doctor to help sick people get better.

I could be a footballer to score a goal with a superb
header.

I could be a pilot, fly a plane taking passengers where
they want to go.

I could be a superstar with amazing talent and
become the star of the show.

I could be a vet who cares for animals of all kinds.

I could be a brain surgeon looking after patients'
minds.

I could be a lawyer fighting for what is right.

I could be a nurse who only works during the night.

When I grow up, what could I be?

How are you feeling after reading When I grow up?

Create your own poem.

A Day Out

"Remember to smile every day."

A Day Out

As we walk along the pathway, everything looks so huge!

We stop at a signpost indicating so many ways to choose.

A giraffe's legs are so tall, the neck even taller.

I see the giraffe looking down at me; I imagine I look smaller.

The monkeys are active, jumping from tree to tree.

I start waving at them, hoping one comes over to say hello to me.

I can't wait to see the lions and listen to them roar.

Lions are my favourite animals; I hope I get to see more than four.

The zoo is filled with different animals, species of every kind.

We had so much fun today; it will be sad to leave them behind.

How are you feeling after reading A Day Out?

Create your own poem.

Thank you for taking the time to read my book.

If you wish to share any of your poems with me, or would like them to be displayed in The Children's Corner on my website, please email your masterpiece to: jaypoems2020@gmail.com

Website: www.jaypoems.co.uk

Printed in Great Britain
by Amazon